CAPTAIN FACT's

SPACE ADVENTURE

BY
KNIFE & PACKER

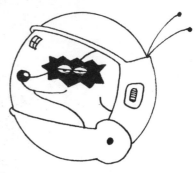

EGMONT

KNIFE & PACKER FACT!

WHEN KNIFE AND PACKER WERE GROWING UP THEY DREAMED OF
ONE DAY GOING INTO SPACE. BUT BY THE TIME THEY WERE OLD
ENOUGH TO BE ASTRONAUTS, THEY COULDN'T SQUEEZE INTO THEIR
SPACE SUITS! SO INSTEAD THEY'VE BEEN WRITING AND DRAWING
TOGETHER EVER SINCE.

First published in Great Britain in 2004
by Egmont Books Limited, 239 Kensington High Street, London W8 6SA

Text and illustrations copyright © 2004 Knife and Packer
The moral rights of the authors have been asserted.

ISBN 1 4052 0832 5

3 5 7 9 10 8 6 4 2

A CIP catalogue record for this title is available
from the British Library

Printed and bound in Great Britain

CONTENTS

STAR

CLIFF THORNHILL
TV'S WORST WEATHERMAN.

PUDDLES
THE ONLY
WEATHERDOG ON TV.

CAPTAIN FACT
THE WORLD'S FIRST
INFORMATION SUPERHERO.

KNOWLEDGE
CAPTAIN FACT'S
FAITHFUL SIDEKICK.

RING...

LUCY
HEAD OF MAKE-UP AND CLIFF'S BEST FRIEND.

THE BOSS
HE'S SCARY!

PROFESSOR MINISCULE
HEAD OF THE FACT CAVE AND THE BRAINS BEHIND MISSIONS.

FACTORELLA
PROFESSOR MINISCULE'S DAUGHTER AND ALL-ROUND WHIZZ-KID.

CHAPTER 1
MONKEY IN SPACE!

IT WAS A typical day for TV's worst weatherman, Cliff Thornhill. He was in the Boss's office getting yet another telling off!

'Yesterday you said it was going to snow!' yelled the Boss.

Luckily for Cliff and Puddles, Cliff's co-presenter and well-meaning companion, the audience loved them.

So even if they did always get the weather wrong the Boss couldn't sack them.

As they returned to their office, Cliff and Puddles noticed a huge crowd gathered round a TV screen.

'There's a monkey on a collision course with Mars!' gasped Lucy, Cliff's friend from the Make-up Department.

'A monkey in space?' asked Cliff.

'It's no ordinary monkey,' explained Lucy. 'That's Dr Barnabas, the world's most intelligent primate. He's on a mission to explore Mars and his spaceship, Ape-ollo 13, has been damaged. He's down to his last two bananas! He can't last much longer!'

Before she'd finished her sentence Cliff and Puddles had run off.

'Strange,' thought Lucy, 'Cliff and Puddles always seem to disappear when there's a crisis ...'

Slightly out of breath, Cliff and Puddles reached their office.

'Right, Cliff, you know what this is ...' said Puddles excitedly. Puddles only spoke when he was alone with Cliff.

'Yes,' said Cliff dramatically. 'THIS IS A ...'

'Stop right there!' shouted Puddles. 'I think you'll find it's my turn to say it.'

'You always say it,' complained Cliff.

'Pleeeeease ...' wheedled Puddles.

'Oh, all right then. But I'm saying it next time,' said Cliff.

And with that Puddles pulled a lever. The portrait of Cliff's great-great-great uncle Sir Phineas Thornhill began to judder, then slowly slid back to reveal a secret tunnel ...

FACT CAVE

13

'Right, Puddles – I mean Knowledge – we've got a long journey ahead of us,' said Captain Fact as they ran through the corridors of the Fact Cave.

'I like long journeys,' said Knowledge, puffing hard, 'shall I pack my swimming trunks?'

'Don't be silly. We're going to Mars to rescue Dr Barnabas.'

'Great! Where do we catch the bus? Or is there a train?' asked Knowledge.

'Don't be ridiculous, Knowledge. We need a spaceship, one with plenty of room for bananas ... we've got a monkey to rescue!'

'But why send a monkey into space?' asked Knowledge as they reached the door to the Fact Cave's Nerve Centre.

'Ker-Fact! Monkeys have been sent into space for years,' said Captain Fact. 'The first monkey in space was called Gordo, back in 1958!'

'But why are they sent?' asked Knowledge.

'At first it was to see whether it was possible to live in space. Now animals help out on all sorts of experiments,' said Captain Fact. 'Hold on to your Fact Mask Knowledge, I feel a Fact Attack coming on . . .' said Captain Fact, as his head began to throb . . .

'Oh,' sighed Knowledge. 'I thought I was going to be the first dog in space.'

'Well,' said Captain Fact as they approached the door of the Nerve Centre, 'you'll be the first *weather* dog in space.'

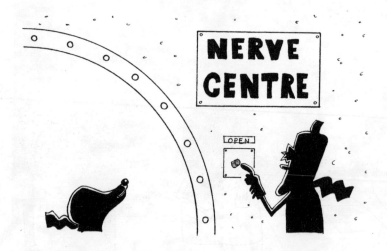

'Great!' said Knowledge. 'But where are we going to find a spaceship to take us there?'

CHAPTER 2
COUNTDOWN

'AH, CAPTAIN FACT and Knowledge, there you are. What kept you?' said Professor Miniscule, the world's shortest genius. Whilst Captain Fact and Knowledge are forecasting the weather as Cliff and Puddles, Professor Miniscule is busily working in the Fact Cave, planning missions and inventing gadgets.

'Getting to Mars isn't going to be easy,' warned Miniscule. 'But I've invented the

super-charged, extra-boosted FactNik1 that can get you there in time to rescue Dr Barnabas.'

Just then Factorella, Professor Miniscule's daughter, rushed in wearing a spanking new spacesuit.

'When do we leave, Dad?' asked Factorella, enthusiastically.

'How many times do I have to tell you? You're too young to go on missions,' said Professor Miniscule. 'You'll have to wait till you're older.'

'But you're always sending me out to rescue Captain Fact and Knowledge when they're in trouble,' moaned Factorella.

'That's part of your training,' said Professor Miniscule, 'just like being in charge of the computers. What have you come up with on space travel?'

'Lots,' said Factorella. She fired up the Fact Cave supercomputer, Factotum.

21

'Don't we have a weather forecast to do?' asked Knowledge, who was beginning to get cold paws.

'I'll go!' shouted Factorella.

'No,' said Professor Miniscule. 'Haven't you got to debug Factotum?'

'Suppose so,' said Factorella, with a sigh.

'Come on, Knowledge,' said Captain Fact. 'Think of Dr Barnabas – the weather can wait.'

'There's no time for chit-chat! Put on these protective space suits, you'll need them for take-off and landing. I've never made one for a dog before – it was quite a challenge,' said Miniscule, as he handed Captain Fact and Knowledge their outfits.

NOT MY COLOUR BUT A PERFECT FIT

'I like the badge,' said
Knowledge.

'Ker-Fact! All space
expeditions have a
specially designed cloth
badge, called a MISSION
BADGE,' said Captain Fact.

'There's no time to waste,'
said Professor Miniscule,
shoving them towards the exit.
'We must hurry to the launch pad,
your spaceship is ready for take-off.'

As they approached the spaceship, Captain
Fact's elbows began to tingle. . .

FACT

FACT
THE SPACE SHUTTLE, FIRST LAUNCHED IN 1981, IS THE FIRST RE-USABLE SPACECRAFT. IT LANDS LIKE A PLANE!

SPACECRAFT

FACT AT BLAST-OFF, ROCKETS CAN REACH TEMPERATURES OF UP TO 3,300°C. THAT'S TWICE THE TEMPERATURE THAT MELTS STEEL!

'You'll find a toolbox full of gadgets in the cockpit for when you get closer to Mars,' said Professor Miniscule. 'And a great, big bag of bananas for Dr Barnabas.'

Captain Fact and Knowledge nervously climbed aboard the spaceship. A few last-minute checks and then it would be lift-off!

SECRET FACT!

SO HOW DOES CAPTAIN FACT KNOW SO MUCH?

WHEN CLIFF THORNHILL WAS SEVEN YEARS OLD HE FELL ASLEEP IN HIS LOCAL LIBRARY ...

AS HE SLEPT A HUGE STORM BREWED UP AND THE LIBRARY WAS STRUCK BY LIGHTNING ...

BLAM!

A GINORMOUS ELECTRIC SHOCK PASSED THROUGH EVERY BOOK AND ZAPPED ALL THE FACTS INTO CLIFF'S BRAIN ...

CHAPTER 3

5
4
3
2
1

BLAST OFF!

AS FACTNIK 1 took off, Captain Fact and Knowledge began to feel strange . . .

'What's going on? I feel all weird and wobbly and my tail's throbbing,' said Knowledge. 'I wonder if it was that minestrone-flavoured dog biscuit I had for breakfast.'

'No. It's because of our fantastic speed,' said Captain Fact.

'But my head feels like a blown-up balloon!' shrieked Knowledge.

'All your fluids are rushing to your head.

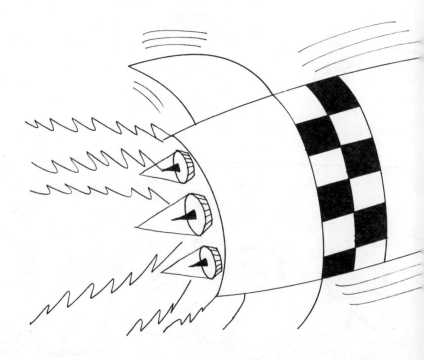

On Earth gravity pulls the body's fluids down towards the toes,' explained Captain Fact.

'I'm not sure if I'm cut out for this astronaut business,' said Knowledge. 'I prefer a nice warm TV studio. How do astronauts cope?'

'Unlike us, they've done years of training,' said Captain Fact.

'Really?' asked Knowledge. 'You mean there's an astronaut school?'

Just then Captain Fact's head started to shudder...

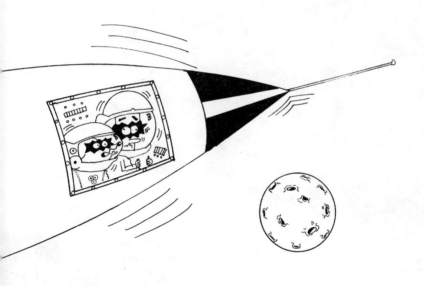

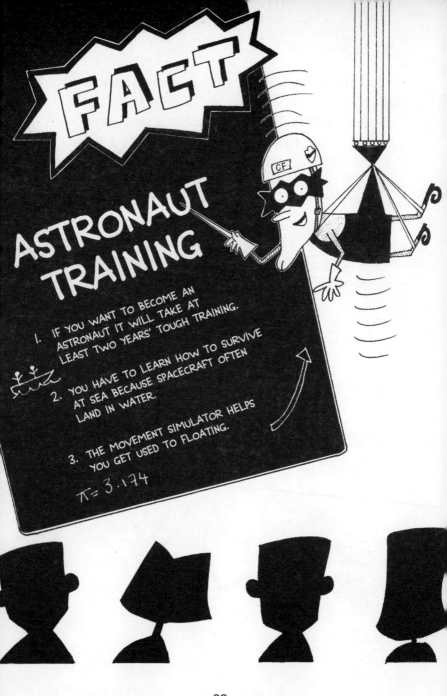

FACT

ASTRONAUT TRAINING

1. IF YOU WANT TO BECOME AN ASTRONAUT IT WILL TAKE AT LEAST TWO YEARS' TOUGH TRAINING.

2. YOU HAVE TO LEARN HOW TO SURVIVE AT SEA BECAUSE SPACECRAFT OFTEN LAND IN WATER.

3. THE MOVEMENT SIMULATOR HELPS YOU GET USED TO FLOATING.

$\pi = 3.174$

After a safe take-off, Captain Fact took the controls to fly the spaceship all the way to Mars.

'This looks easy,' said Knowledge. 'Space is completely empty – there's no traffic lights, no roundabouts, no pedestrians. Let me have a go.'

'That's just where you're wrong,' said Captain Fact, as he handed the controls to Knowledge. 'Look out of the window, space is full of stuff – rocks, dust, satellites. Ker-Fact! There are at least 1,000 working satellites zooming around the Earth.

AND WE'RE HEADING FOR ONE RIGHT NOW!' he
added, struggling to stay calm as he grabbed back
the controls. 'I'll steer, you make contact with Dr
Barnabas.'

Knowledge tweaked the dials and fiddled with
the buttons and eventually a crackly picture
popped up on the video screen.

'... *fizzzz* – come in please – *crackle* – I'm off
course – *pop* – fuel low, banana levels critical –
crackle – are you receiving me?'

'Did you hear that, Captain Fact? Banana levels
are critical – hit the boosters!

Captain Fact and Knowledge cranked the spaceship up to top speed. Carefully avoiding satellites, they began the longest and most dangerous part of their journey – flying beyond the Moon to Mars.

'There's still about 77.348 million kilometres to go,' said Captain Fact. 'It's going to take a while. You'd better get used to living in space, Knowledge. And in the meantime, Factorella has provided us with Factotum's Fact File on the planets.'

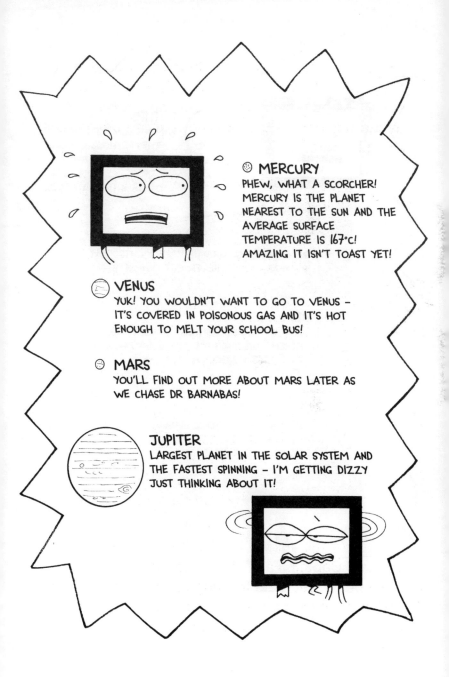

☺ MERCURY
PHEW, WHAT A SCORCHER! MERCURY IS THE PLANET NEAREST TO THE SUN AND THE AVERAGE SURFACE TEMPERATURE IS 167°C! AMAZING IT ISN'T TOAST YET!

☺ VENUS
YUK! YOU WOULDN'T WANT TO GO TO VENUS – IT'S COVERED IN POISONOUS GAS AND IT'S HOT ENOUGH TO MELT YOUR SCHOOL BUS!

⊖ MARS
YOU'LL FIND OUT MORE ABOUT MARS LATER AS WE CHASE DR BARNABAS!

JUPITER
LARGEST PLANET IN THE SOLAR SYSTEM AND THE FASTEST SPINNING – I'M GETTING DIZZY JUST THINKING ABOUT IT!

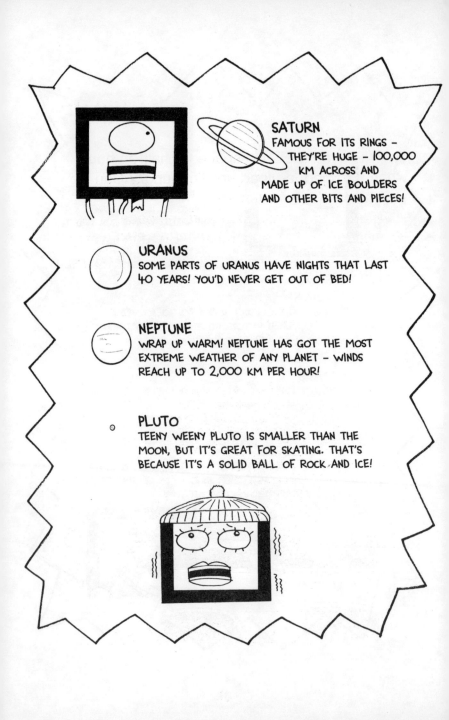

SATURN
FAMOUS FOR ITS RINGS – THEY'RE HUGE – 100,000 KM ACROSS AND MADE UP OF ICE BOULDERS AND OTHER BITS AND PIECES!

URANUS
SOME PARTS OF URANUS HAVE NIGHTS THAT LAST 40 YEARS! YOU'D NEVER GET OUT OF BED!

NEPTUNE
WRAP UP WARM! NEPTUNE HAS GOT THE MOST EXTREME WEATHER OF ANY PLANET – WINDS REACH UP TO 2,000 KM PER HOUR!

PLUTO
TEENY WEENY PLUTO IS SMALLER THAN THE MOON, BUT IT'S GREAT FOR SKATING. THAT'S BECAUSE IT'S A SOLID BALL OF ROCK AND ICE!

CHAPTER 4
POWDERED PINEAPPLE

THEY'D ONLY BEEN in space for half an hour when Knowledge piped up, 'I'm hungry. Can we stop somewhere for lunch?'

'There aren't any restaurants in space, Knowledge,' said Captain Fact. 'But don't worry, Professor Miniscule has provided us with some wonderful space food.'

'Great!' said Knowledge. 'I'll have a chilli-flavoured dog biscuit covered in gravy and a strawberry one for pud.'

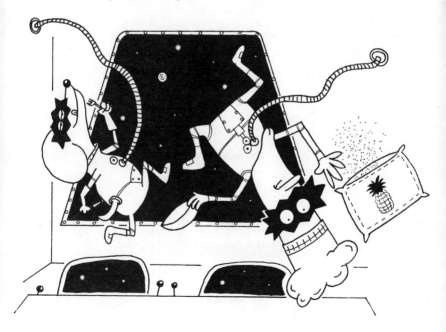

'I'm afraid food's not like that out here,' said Captain Fact. 'Ker-Fact! Everything you eat in space has to be specially packaged. Tuck in to this dried pear and powdered pineapple. Yum!'

'Yuk! I think I'll wait until we get back to Earth,' said Knowledge. 'I'm off to the little dog's room. Is it through here?'

'No! That's the emergency escape hatch, don't open that! There's the toilet, over there.'

'That giant vacuum cleaner? How does that work?'

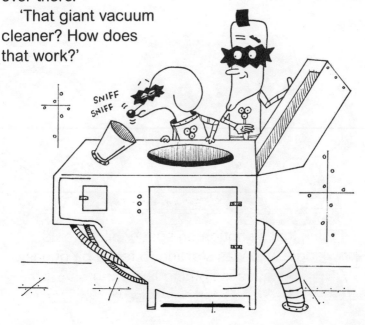

SNIFF
SNIFF

'Let me explain,' said Captain Fact, 'You need some space toilet facts . . . Because of weightlessness, a conventional toilet would lead to all manner of things floating around. After all, you wouldn't want to bump into a poo, would you? Basically the toilet *is* a giant vacuum cleaner – it sucks everything up. Your pee is even recycled into drinking water and oxygen!'

'I think that's enough on space toilets,' said Knowledge, who was starting to feel a bit queasy.
'Living in space is nothing like living on Earth,' said Captain Fact as his nose began to twitch . . .

'... *crackle* – Fact Cave calling FactNik 1, come in please, this is Professor Miniscule calling!'

'Great,' said Knowledge. 'I wanted to have a word with you. About this space food – it's horrible! Is there any chance of sending up some dog biscuits? And as for the space toilet . . .'

'There's no time for that – *fizz* – you're on a collision course with a meteor!'

CHAPTER 5
BUMP!

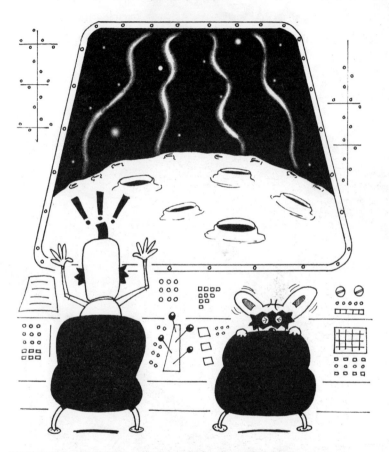

'BELT UP, KNOWLEDGE! This could get bumpy,'
warned Captain Fact as he scrambled to his seat.
  'What's a meteor?' asked Knowledge.
  Captain Fact's ears began to wobble . . .

48

'We've been knocked miles off course. All our communication systems are out of action,' said Captain Fact dusting himself down.

'I'm beginning to realise how Dr Barnabas must feel,' said Knowledge. 'At least we've got lots of bananas ...'

'Don't even think about eating those. We're on a mission here, and we're not going to fail. We've just got to get out of this pickle,' said Captain Fact.

When Captain Fact and Knowledge find themselves in a particularly sticky pickle they use one of Professor Miniscule's most brilliant inventions: the Fact Watch. Captain Fact pressed the emergency button and Miniscule's face appeared.

'Miniscule, we have a problem,' said Captain Fact.

'I know,' said the Professor, 'I've been tracking your progress and I've sent Factorella.'

Suddenly FactNik 1 began to shudder and there was a huge bang. Knowledge looked out of the window ...

'There's a spaceship coming straight for us!' With a flash, Factorella appeared.

'Wow! This is great!' said Factorella. 'Space is brilliant! Now, Dad's told me exactly what to do ...

I'm going to tow you to the nearest space station to get the ship repaired. Knowledge, you like walkies, don't you?'

'Yes,' replied Knowledge, who actually preferred barbeque-flavoured dog biscuits.

'Well, get your space suit on: you're going *space* walkies. I need you to tie this rope to the front of your ship.

'Ker-Fact! Work outside a spaceship is called "Extra Vehicular Activity",' said Captain Fact as Knowledge prepared to leave FactNik 1.

And so Knowledge became the first dog ever
to walk in space. When he'd attached the rope,
Factorella was able to pull their broken-down
spaceship through the Asteroid Belt to the
space station.

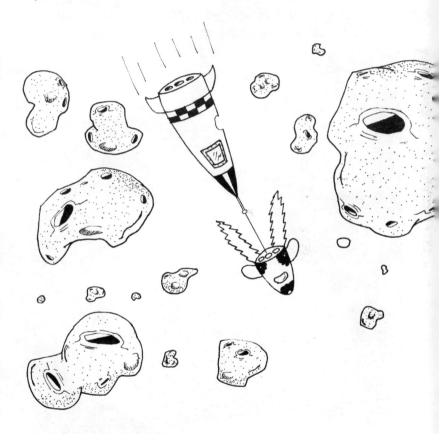

As they passed through the Asteroid Belt,
Captain Fact's toes began to tingle ...

'Look, Knowledge, the space station!' said Captain Fact as Factorella guided them to the docking hatch.

'I'd love to stick around, but I had to promise to go straight back,' said Factorella as she zoomed off.

'Goodbye, Factorella,' called Captain Fact, 'and thank you!'

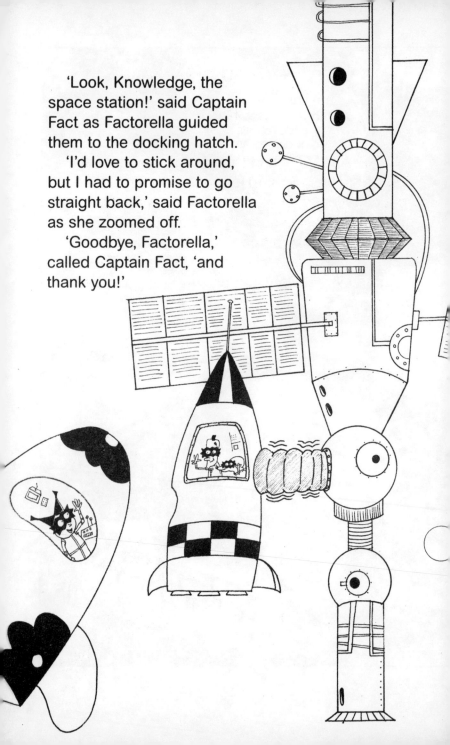

CHAPTER 6
BORIS

AS CAPTAIN FACT and Knowledge, now smartly dressed in their Super-Hero outfits, boarded the space station, a large, unshaven cosmonaut greeted them. He scooped up both Captain Fact and Knowledge in a huge bear hug.

'Hello, hello! I'm Cosmonaut Boris and I'm so delighted to see you! You are my first visitors in three years!'

'I can't breath!' wheezed Knowledge.

'You're squashing my cape,' gasped Captain Fact.

'Professor Miniscule has told me all about your encounter with a meteor. It shouldn't take long to repair the ship,' said Boris. 'It'll make a nice change from endless experiments. That's all I do out here – eat, sleep and conduct experiments ...'

'We've never been on a space station before,' said Knowledge, straightening his cape.

As Boris got to work repairing FactNik 1, Captain Fact and Knowledge started to explore.

'It's like being in a giant train carriage,' said Knowledge.

'It's a bit more complicated than that, Knowledge,' said Captain Fact as his knees began to tremble . . .

FACT

FACT
SPACE STATIONS CAN GROW!
EXTRA MODULES CAN BE
ADDED — A BIT LIKE BUILDING
AN EXTENSION ON THE BACK
OF YOUR HOUSE!

FACT
THE MIR SPACE STATION
HAS BEEN IN ORBIT
SINCE 1986 AND IS USED
FOR EXPERIMENTS ON
SPACE AND SPACE LIFE.

SPACE STATION

'Your ship is repaired and ready to go – I've even fitted extra boosters!' said Cosmonaut Boris. 'Now, are you sure you can't stick around? It's just that I get so lonely all on my own up here. We could play chess, listen to pop music . . . I've even got some powdered cabbage!'

'Sorry, Cosmonaut Boris, but we really must go,' said Knowledge.

'We can't leave Dr Barnabas any longer,' said Captain Fact.

'I understand. Good luck! And if you're ever near the space station, don't be a stranger.'

Without further ado Captain Fact and Knowledge fired up FactNik 1.

CHAPTER 7
DESTINATION MARS

ONCE AGAIN CAPTAIN Fact and Knowledge were hurtling through space towards Mars.

'... *crackle* – Professor Miniscule here – *fizz* – come in FactNik 1!'

'FactNik 1 here' replied Captain Fact.

'... *crackle* – with those incredibly powerful boosters that Cosmonaut Boris fitted – *pop* - you should be approaching Mars shortly.'

'At last ... Mars,' said Captain Fact as the tip of his nose began to twitch.

FACT

MARTIAN DUST STORMS OCCASIONALLY GET REALLY UGLY AND CAN COVER THE ENTIRE PLANET FOR MONTHS.

FACT

MARS MIGHT LOOK HOT BUT IT'S ACTUALLY FREEZING COLD. THAT'S BECAUSE IT'S MUCH FURTHER FROM THE SUN THAN THE EARTH.

FACT

THE SAME CHEMICAL THAT MAKES RUST RED – IRON OXIDE – GIVES MARS ITS STRIKING COLOUR. AND ITS NICKNAME – 'THE RED PLANET'.

As Captain Fact and Knowledge approached
Mars, a small dot suddenly appeared on the radar.
It was getting bigger every second . . .

'It's Ape-ollo 13! We're going to save Dr
Barnabas!' cried Knowledge.

'Not so fast, Knowledge,' said Captain Fact. 'I
think he's going to . . .

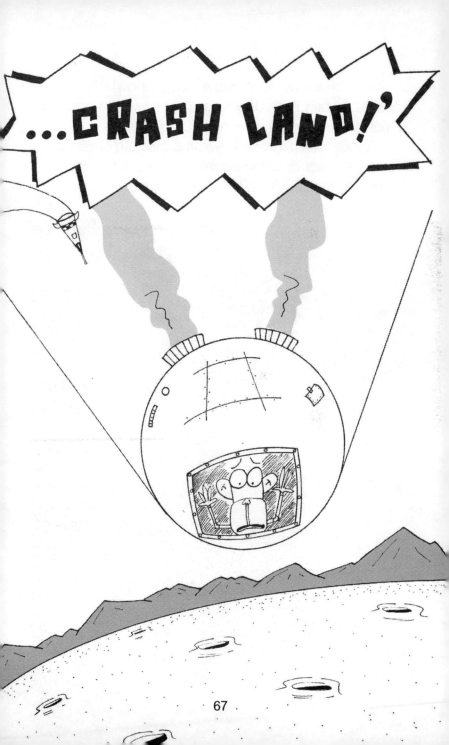

. . . You know what this means, Knowledge,'
said Captain Fact. 'We're going to have to land on
Mars! I'll steer, you find a landing spot.'

As FactNik 1 roared over the Martian surface,
Captain Fact couldn't resist pointing out some of
Mars's amazing features.

At last they found a safe place to land.
'Great landing spot, Knowledge!' said Captain Fact.

'There's just one problem,' said Knowledge, peering at the instruments, 'Dr Barnabas is two kilometres away!'

CHAPTER 8
GOING BANANAS

'RIGHT, MARTIAN SPACESUITS on. There's no time to waste,' said Captain Fact, reaching into Professor Miniscule's toolbox of gadgets.

'Wouldn't it be quicker without these bulky suits?' asked Knowledge. 'They weigh a tonne.'

'You can't walk around a place as inhospitable as Mars without a spacesuit on!' said Captain Fact, as his earlobes began to wobble . . .

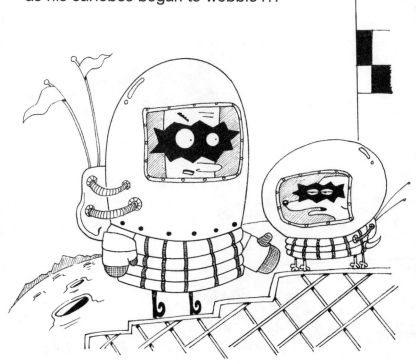

FACT

FACT
ON SPACEWALKS,
ASTRONAUTS WEAR A
PRIMARY LIFE-SUPPORT SUB-
SYSTEM. IT'S LIKE A HIGH-
TECH BACKPACK AND IT
PROVIDES OXYGEN AND
COMMUNICATION WITH THE
SPACESHIP, AND KEEPS THE
TEMPERATURE STEADY.

FACT
A SPACESUIT IS LIKE A
PROTECTIVE SHELL THAT
PROTECTS THE ASTRONAUT
FROM ALL THE NASTY
STUFF IN SPACE: FREEZING
COLD, BOILING HEAT,
GHASTLY GASES.

FACT
THE VISOR ON THE
HELMET IS COATED
WITH GOLD TO REFLECT
HEAT AND LIGHT.

SPACE SUITS

After twenty minutes of staggering and stumbling across Mars's rocky surface, Captain Fact and Knowledge were getting nowhere fast.

'We're never going to get to Dr Barnabas in time,' sighed Knowledge. 'I can hardly move in this thing. Isn't there a gadget in Professor Miniscule's toolbox that will speed things up?'

'I'll have a look,' said Captain Fact, waddling back to FactNik 1. After a bit of rummaging around, Captain Fact emerged with a space vehicle. 'Ker-Fact! The Sojourner robot buggy was specially designed to explore the surface of Mars and travels at 40 centimetres per minute. Fortunately, this one's been turbo-charged by Professor Miniscule. We'll be with Dr Barnabas in no time,' he said, jumping onboard.

As they set off, Captain Fact noticed that Knowledge was covering his eyes.

'I'm worried we might meet some little green men,' said Knowledge.

'You've been reading too much science fiction' said Captain Fact, as his chin began to wobble ...

FACT

FACT
PEOPLE HAVE ALWAYS WONDERED WHETHER THERE IS LIFE ON MARS. EARLY ASTRONOMERS THOUGHT THEY COULD SEE CANALS ON MARS!

FACT
THERE HAVE BEEN LOADS OF FILMS, BOOKS AND COMICS FILLED WITH SCARY STORIES ABOUT MARTIANS.

THE MOST FAMOUS IS H. G. WELLS'S 'WAR OF THE WORLDS' WHICH HAS BEEN SCARING PEOPLE SINCE 1898.

AMAZING STORIES

LIFE ON MARS

FACT

BEFORE YOU GET TOO SCARED ABOUT CREATURES FROM MARS TURNING UP AT YOUR HOUSE, YOU'LL BE PLEASED TO HEAR FROM VIKINGS I AND II. THESE UNMANNED SPACE PROBES LANDED ON MARS IN 1976 AND FOUND NO SIGN OF LIFE. PHEW!

HIDE!

THIS ISN'T THE END OF THE STORY, THOUGH. IN 1984 A METEORITE FROM MARS WAS DISCOVERED IN ANTARCTICA. IT HAD STRANGE SHAPES IN IT. ARE THEY FOSSILS FROM ANCIENT MARTIAN LIFE FORMS?

ATTACK!!!

With their Robot Buggy in top gear, Captain Fact and Knowledge were soon in sight of Dr Barnabas.

'Hang on, Dr Barnabas, we'll soon be with you!' shouted Captain Fact. 'And we've got bananas!'

And so, after a death-defying journey, Captain
Fact and Knowledge finally reached Dr Barnabas ...

'Its great to see you! I knew you'd make it!
Mmmm ...' said Dr Barnabas as he tucked into his
fifteenth banana.

'There's no time to waste,' said Captain Fact,
'we're running out of oxygen – we've got to get
back to Earth!'

CHAPTER 9
MONKEY ON BOARD

WITH THE WORLD'S most intelligent primate firmly strapped in, Captain Fact and Knowledge blasted off and began the descent to Earth.

'We'll have you back in no time, Dr Barnabas,' said Captain Fact. 'All we have to do is avoid the satellites, asteroids and meteors we ran into on the way to Mars.'

'Talking of space junk, look at the size of that,' said Knowledge.

'That's not space junk, that's the Moon,' explained Captain Fact. His nostrils were twitching again . . .

FACT

FACT

A VERY UNLUCKY MOON MISSION WAS APOLLO 13 IN 1970. AN ONBOARD EXPLOSION MEANT THE CREW HAD TO MAKE EMERGENCY REPAIRS BEFORE A SPEEDY AND SAFE RETURN TO EARTH.

FACT

A FOOTPRINT LEFT BY AN ASTRONAUT WILL BE THERE FOR EVER. THAT'S BECAUSE THERE'S NO WIND OR RAIN TO DISTURB IT.

THE MOON

'We're heading straight for it!' screamed Dr Barnabas.

'Hit the brakes!' shouted Captain Fact, yanking back on his control stick as hard as he could.

At the last second FactNik 1 screeched away from the Moon's surface.

'That was close!' said Knowledge, helping Dr Barnabas back into his seat.

'Almost too close,' said Captain Fact.

Having narrowly avoided the Moon, the ship began to rattle and shake.

'What's going on now?' asked Knowledge, 'I'm getting that wobbly feeling again!'

'It's quite normal,' said Captain Fact, whose mask had gone skew-whiff.

'Let me explain what's happening, Knowledge,' piped up Dr Barnabas from the back seat.

'Hold it right there, Dr Barnabas!' interrupted Captain Fact. 'I do the facts around here. Ker-Fact! We're re-entering the Earth's atmosphere. This means that the ship's under huge pressure, and that's why you're feeling strange, Knowledge.'

'...*crackle* – FactNik 1 this is Professor Miniscule – *fizz* – you're coming into land – *crackle* – you'll need to splash down in water.'

'We're over the Pacific,' said Dr Barnabas. 'I know this great island we could land near – beautiful beaches, glorious sunsets and all the bananas you can eat!'

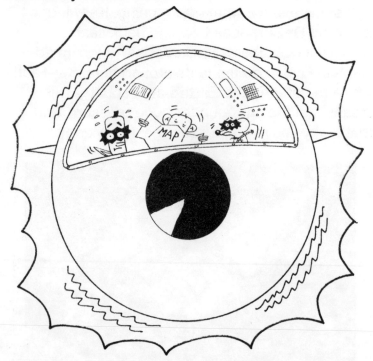

'There's no time for that, Dr Barnabas,' said Captain Fact as he clung on to the controls of the shaking spaceship. 'We've got an evening weather forecast to present...'

CHAPTER 10
AND NOW THE WEATHER ...

'WHAT ABOUT THE city swimming pool?'
suggested Knowledge.

'It's an *indoor* pool,' replied Captain Fact.

'How about the aquarium?' suggested
Dr Barnabas.

'That's got sharks,' said Captain Fact.

'The park!' exclaimed Knowledge.

'It's got a pond,' said Captain Fact, 'let's do it!'

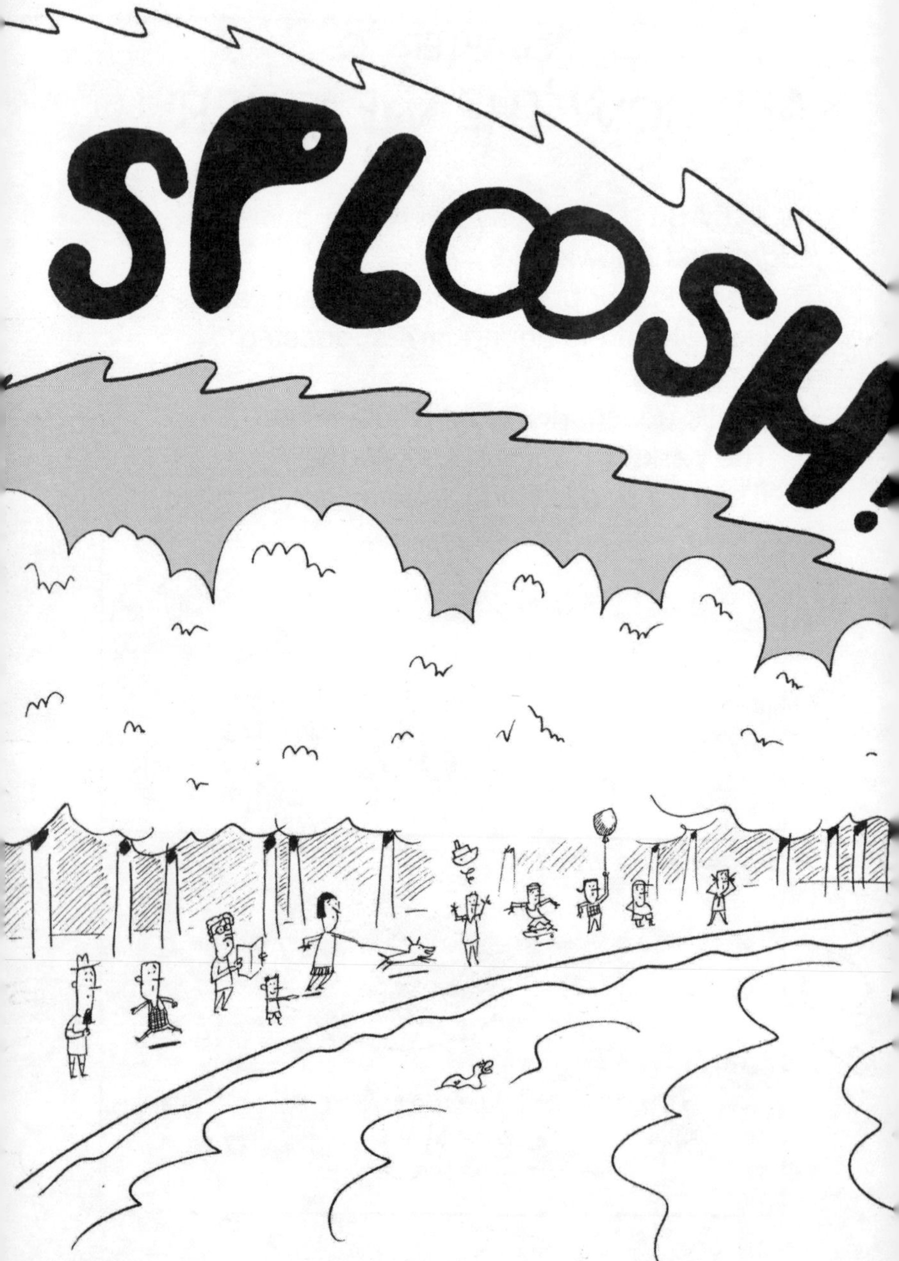
SPLOOSH!

'We've done it!' shouted Captain Fact, as the ship bobbed to the surface.

'Home at last,' said Knowledge. 'I can't wait to tuck into some proper food – custard-flavoured dog biscuits here I come!'

'Thank you, Captain Fact and Knowledge,' said Dr Barnabas. 'I'm on a mission to Saturn next week. Why don't you come along?'

'I think we'll be staying on Earth, thank you, Dr Barnabas,' said Captain Fact. Just then he realised that a huge crowd had gathered. 'We'd better slip away, our identities must remain a secret,' he said.

Captain Fact and Knowledge didn't even have time to get changed as they rushed into the TV studio. In fact, they only just had time to get their masks off . . .

'We've made it!' said Captain Fact as he crashed into the boss.

'Where on earth have you been, and why are you wearing those ridiculous spacesuits?' demanded the boss.

'We've been to . . . er . . . um . . . a fancy dress party!' blurted Captain Fact.

'Well, it's one minute to six. Get changed and get to the studio. NOW!' screamed the Boss.

Pulling their spacesuits off as they ran down the corridors of the TV studio, Captain Fact and Knowledge burst through the doors to the Make-up Department.

'Ah, Cliff and Puddles, there you are,' said Lucy. 'Have you heard the news? Dr Barnabas has been rescued!'

'Really?' said Cliff, pretending not to know anything about it, 'who by?'

'Captain Fact and Knowledge,' said Lucy. 'I'd love to meet Captain Fact, he's my hero.'

'Er . . . um . . .' said Cliff blushing.

'Come on, Cliff,' whispered Puddles, 'we've got the weather to do.'

And so, with Dr Barnabas safely back on Earth, Cliff Thornhill and Puddles were back doing what they did worst – the weather.

Until the next crisis . . .

COMING SOON!

CAPTAIN FACT's

DINOSAUR ADVENTURE

CREEPY CRAWLY ADVENTURE

EGYPTIAN ADVENTURE

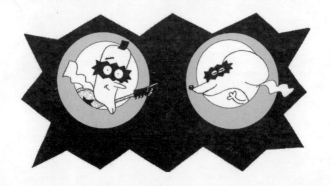